The Journey

A recipe book for those who have gastrointestinal issues.

THERESA FOCHTMAN

To order additional copies of this book, contact:
Xlibris
844-714-8691
www.Xlibris.com
Orders@Xlibris.com

ISBN: Softcover   979-8-3694-1851-2
             Hardcover   979-8-3694-1852-9
             EBook   979-8-3694-1850-5

Library of Congress Control Number: 2024905969

Print information available on the last page

Rev. date: 03/25/2024

Avocado Salad

Now when it comes to fruits and vegetables, there are certain ones that I can eat as long as they are prepared in a certain way. This is an easy recipe that should not hurt your stomach.

minerals which is something that we do not get enough of.

 Serves 1 person

Ingredients

 1 soft avocado

 4 tbsp mayo

 Salt and pepper to taste

Instructions

- Slice your avocado in half. Cut into chunks. Make sure that there is no pulp and or hard shell on the avocado.

- Put the chunks in a bowl

- Add the mayo

- Lightly mix the mayo and avocado together. You still want there to be some chunkiness to it.

That's it. Pretty simple. At times I will add a little cilantro oil and garlic powder to change it up a bit.

This also goes well with white toast or toasted sourdough.

Avocados are full of good fats, and are low in saturated fats. They include 20 vitamins and

Give me that Spicy Chicken!

I love this recipe because you can make so much with it. You can make shredded chicken tacos, shredded chicken sliders, shredded chicken nachos

I eat a lot of chicken because it is very easy for my body to digest. This recipe is also made in the crock pot. You really want to give the chicken time to marry and time for it to cook so it is easy to shred.

Ingredients

 Usually, I am cooking for 4 people. If you are cooking for more than 4, please double the recipe.

- 1 pack of skinless and boneless chicken thighs.
- 2 tbsp infused Chipotle Garlic olive oil. (can purchase at Oil and Vinegar or Celia's online)
- 1 tbsp garlic powder
- 1 tbsp onion powder
- ½ tbsp slap ya mamas seasoning
- ½ tbsp greek seasoning
- 2 tbsp worcestershire sauce
- ½ tbsp Sriracha
- 10 oz chicken broth

Instructions

- Turn your crockpot on high

- Add your chicken broth to the crock pot

- In a bowl add your skinless boneless chicken thighs

- Mix all of the ingredients together.

- Add all of the ingredients to the crock pot.

You are going to let the chicken cook for 2 hours. After that, give it a quick stir. If the chicken is looking dry, add some more chicken broth to the crock pot. At hour 3 take a fork and a knife to the chicken. At that point you should be able to shred the chicken pretty easily. All crock pots are not the same. My crock pot is pretty old, so it does take a bit longer to cook. Your shredded chicken should be ready to eat in 3 to 4 hours.

I like to take a soft flour tortilla shell and cook it on the stove top for a few minutes. I'll add a little olive oil, so the shell is soft. Once the shell is cooked, I put it on a plate and add my shredded chicken to the shell. I add sour cream and some cheese. You can add any cheese that you like.

If I am making sliders, I buy the Hawaiian buns sliders that you can purchase at your local grocery store. I cut the sliders in half and put them in the broiler for a few minutes until they get crispy. I add Mayo and Swiss cheese to one side of the bun and then add the shredded chicken and close the bun.

This recipe is awesome for family dinner and football games. It may take time for it to cook but once it's done, you slap it on a bun or taco shell and you are good to go!

Fun fact. Olive oil is very healthy for you. Olive oil is good for heart health. Most people who live in the Mediterranean use olive oil. It's easy to digest and has many benefits for your body unlike other seed oils.

Ground Chicken Meatballs

I love this recipe because you can make meatball subs and fettuccine alfredo. I like to make extra so I can prepare meals for a couple of days. You may choose gluten free and dairy free options.

Ingredients

- 1 pound ground chicken
- 1 egg
- ½ cup panko bread crumbs (may be gluten free)
- ½ grated parmesan cheese (may be dairy free)
- 2 tbsp infused garlic oil (Oil and Vinegar and Celia's online)
- 1 tbsp onion powder
- 2 tsp Worcestershire sauce
- 1-2 tsp salt
- Ground fine black pepper to taste (optional)
- You can add any other seasonings that you may like

Instructions

- Preheat oven to 400f (204c)

- Mix all of the ingredients together in a large mixing bowl

- Roll the mixture into about 30 small balls. Place on a baking sheet.

- Bake the meatballs for 25 to 30 minutes

- After you pull the meatballs out of the oven you can sprinkle some extra parmesan cheese on top.

- And there you have it!

Ain't Your Mama's Chicken Sausage

I know with all of my gastro issues that I cannot eat just any sausage. No pork, no beef, no casing around it.

Ingredients

- 1 pound ground chicken
- 1 large egg
- 2 tsp of infused garlic and cilantro (Oil and Vinegar carries this and Cellia's does as well online)
- 2 tsp Worcestershire sauce
- 2 tsp slap ya mama seasoning (most grocery stores carry this)
- 2 tsp garlic powder

Instructions

- In a mixing bowl combine all of your ingredients together. You are going to make these into patties. I can usually get 4 out of one pound. You can make larger ones or smaller ones.

- Add about 2 tsp of Olive oil to your frying pan. Depending on the size of your patties, I will usually cook mine on medium for about 15 minutes. Flipping them at the halfway point. I

spices listed above. When the sausage patties are done, splash some extra Worcestershire sauce in the pan and let it sit for about a minute. That's it!

This was one of the first recipes that I played with after I was told that I could start eating again. There are no chunks of veggies, nothing extremely fatty. There are no big chunks of spices. This sausage truly made me smile after I got my recipe down. Not being able to eat the delicious food that everyone else can was depressing me. Now I can have flavor in my food, I know what is going into my body and I do not have to worry if I am going to have a bowel obstruction. I can eat without worry. I hope that you love this recipe and that it brings a smile to your face!

Anchovy Spaghetti

This is an Italian favorite. I absolutely love Anchovies. Now, not all spaghetti is created the same. There are a lot of people out there that cannot eat gluten. When you purchase your pasta, please make sure that it is made with Semolina. Semolina is made in Italy. You can buy this type of pasta at any grocery store. You can switch to gluten free pasta if need be. If you decide to choose a gluten free option, please follow the cooking instructions on the package.

 This recipe serves 8

Ingredients

- 1 pound spaghetti
- 4 tbsp olive oil
- 1 (2 ounce) can anchovy filets, chopped
- 3 tbsp infused garlic oil (Oil and Vinegar and Celia's online)
- 2/3 cup fine breadcrumbs, or to taste
- 4 tbsp freshly grated Parmesan cheese

Instructions

- Bring a large pot of salted water and 1 tsp olive oil to a boil. Add pasta and cook for 8 to 10 minutes or until al dente; drain. Do not rinse pasta.

- Heat olive oil in a medium skillet over medium heat. Add anchovies and garlic oil; cook and stir continuously until anchovies' sizzle and garlic is fragrant, about 2 minutes.

- Stir in breadcrumbs and turn off heat.

- Toss anchovy sauce with hot pasta and sprinkle with Parmesan cheese; serve.

Semolina pasta is high in protein, fiber, iron, and vit B. When I went to Italy, I was able to eat the pasta because it was made from Semolina. I am very careful with what types of pasta I can eat. Multi grain pasta is not my friend. It has slowed my bowels down and even created a bowel obstruction. Keep that in mind when you are choosing the pasta that you are going to eat.

Baked Potato Fries with Homemade Fry Sauce

When I found out that I could eat potatoes I literally cried. The one big thing for us with gut issues is that you can not have any skin on the potatoes. If you keep the skin on, there's a big chance you will get a bowel obstruction. So, make sure you peel those potatoes!

Ingredients

- 2 pounds of baking potatoes, I love yellow and russets.
- 2 tbsp infused cilantro olive oil (Oil and Vinegar and Celia's online)
- 1/2 tsp garlic powder
- 1/2 tsp onion powder
- 1/2 tsp cavender's greek seasoning (any store has this)
- salt to taste. I love my salty fries.

Instructions

- Preheat your oven to 450 F (230 C)

- Skin and cut your potatoes into wedges

- Put your potatoes in a large bowl, add seasonings and mix very well.

I put parchment paper on my baking sheet. Add the wedges to the baking sheet. I cook mine for 40 minutes. I flip them halfway through. I love my crispy fries. If you do not, bake them for 15 minutes each side.

On to the Fry sauce.

Ingredients

- 1 cup mayo
- 2 tbsp ketchup
- 1 tbsp mustard
- 1/2 tbsp sriracha
- 1 tbsp dill pickle juice. Make sure it's only the juice no seeds or pulp.
- 1/2 tsp slap ya mama seasoning

Instructions

In a bowl mix all of the ingredients. And there you have it. Amazing fries with one of the best fry sauces you will have ever had.

Put your fries on a plate and your sauce in a little dish. My husband loves this sauce so much that I put it on his sandwiches.

Something easy to make and easy for your stomach. You can always add or remove spices you may or may not like later.

Chicken thigh glazed donut sandwich/burger

Whenever my husband and his friends are out in the shop I make them this for lunch. They absolutely love it. This is a top request at home. You may choose gluten free and dairy free options.

 Serves 4-5 people

Ingredients

- 4-5 boneless and skinless chicken thighs
- 1 tbsp olive oil
- 1 ½ tbsp garlic powder
- 1 tbsp onion powder
- 1 tbsp slap ya mama seasoning (most grocery stores sell this)
- 4 tbsp worcestershire sauce
- Mayo (as much or as little as you'd like)
- 4-5 Glazed donuts (cut in half) each side makes the bun
- Sliced swiss cheese

Instructions

- Add all of the ingredients into a larger mixing bowl.

- In a skillet or frying pan add 1 tbsp oil pan. Have the temperature on medium heat. Once the oil is warmed up, add the chicken. Cook each side for 12 minutes. After the 12 minutes flip. If the sauce starts to dry add in a little water. 1 minute before you pull the chicken off, add your slice of swiss cheese to the chicken thigh. Let it melt a little.

- Cut your glazed donut in half. On one side add the mayo. Place chicken on top and add the next slice of glazed donut.

This is a sweet, savory and spicy burger/sandwich all in one. Your taste buds will not wonder for anything else!

Days Breakfast

My daughter loves my cooking. Whenever she asks mama to cook, I am on it. Just hearing her say "This is soooo good," means the world to me. You may opt for gluten free and dairy free options.

 Serves 1

Ingredients

- 1 cup veined and peeled shrimp (can but frozen or fresh)
- 1 large egg
- 1 tbsp olive oil
- 1 half english muffin
- 1 tbsp butter
- 1 tbsp Infused cilantro oil (Oil and Vinegar and Celia's online)
- Pinch of salt and finely ground black pepper.
- 1 tbsp infused chipotle and garlic oil (Oil and Vinegar and Celia's online)
- 1 tsp Slap ya Mama's seasoning (any local store)

Instructions

- You can choose to cook this recipe with either frozen shrimp or fresh shrimp.

- In a mixing bowl add all of the ingredients. Cover in the fridge for a few minutes.

- In a large skillet add 1 tbsp. olive oil

- Add in the seasoned shrimp

- Sauté shrimp for 2 to 3 minutes.

- Fresh shrimp takes about 2 to 4 minutes. This all depends on the size of the shrimp. The bigger the shrimp, the longer it takes.

- In another frying pan, add a little olive oil of butter of your choosing. Add the one large egg and let the egg cook for about 2-3 minutes. Pull off the burner.

- Toast your English muffin however you like it toasted. I love mine very crispy. After the muffin is toasted add your butter, egg and shrimp.

You get the protein, carbs and good fats that you need. I call this Day's breakfast because my baby girl's name is DayLynn and I call her day. She is the light of my life so I figured why not name a recipe after her!

Did you say Chicken Thighs in a sandwich?

Chicken is one of the easiest foods for someone with Crohn's disease, Gut Motility issues and gastroparesis. This chicken thigh sandwich will have your taste buds watering. You may choose gluten and dairy free options.

Ingredients

 I usually buy a 4 pack of boneless and skinless chicken thighs. If you are feeding more than 3 or 4 people, double up on the spices.

- 1 pack (4) boneless and skinless chicken thighs
- 2 tbsp olive oil
- 1/2 tbsp garlic powder
- 1/2 tbsp onion powder
- 1 tbsp worcestershire sauce
- 1/2 tbsp soy sauce
- 1/2 tbsp slap ya mama seasoning
- 4 slices of sourdough bread (can change to gluten free)

1/2 stick of butter. I usually use vegan butter as real butter does not sit well with me. You can use any butter that you like.

Cut off any extra skin that may be on the chicken thighs.

Instructions

- In a large bowl, add your chicken and all of the ingredients minus the butter. Once the ingredients are added, cover the chicken and put it in the fridge to marinate for about an hour. If I know what I am making I will let it marinate all night. The longer you marinate the more flavors will have time to marry.

- In a skillet or frying pan, add in 3 tbsp of water and 2 tbsp olive oil. Let the pan heat up. I usually have my heat in medium.

- Add your chicken to the skillet or frying pan. Now you want to keep an eye on the chicken because you do not want it to burn. I usually cook fine for about 15 to 20 minutes. When the sauce of the pan dries out, that's when you want to add your butter.

- After your chicken thighs are done, pull them to the side and cover them.

- Sourdough bread is one of the best foods for us to eat. The sourdough kills most of the gluten therefore making it easy to digest. Make sure that when you are looking for sourdough bread that it has a sourdough starter in the ingredient list. Otherwise, it's not a true sourdough bread.

- Turn your broiler on high. If you are making 4 sandwiches, you'll need 8 slices of bread. I put a little coat of olive oil on the bread, broil the bread for about 2 minutes. You want the bread crispy. Not burnt. After there is a little crisp to it, flip it over and crisp the other side. Once the bread is crispy, pull it out of the oven and set aside.

- Now to the good part. I love Mayo and Gorgonzola. I am Italian. What can I say? I love cheese. Known fact, the older the cheese, the better it is to digest. I do not have gut issues with this cheese.

- I buy Crumbled Gorgonzola at Safeway. Most places will carry it. If you are not a mayo fan, you don't need to add it but, it sure makes it better.

- Add mayo and gorgonzola to one side of the bread. The more the better I say! Put your chicken thigh on the side with the mayo and cheese. Put another slice of bread on top. And there you have it! My family and I eat this once or twice a week. You get healthy fats, and the carbs that you need. For me, I was extremely malnourished because I couldn't eat. This will give you nutrients that your body needs.

Garlic Parmesan Focaccia Bread

You may choose the gluten and dairy free option. If you choose to go with gluten free flour, please read the directions on the packaging.

 Serves about 12 people

Ingredients

- 3 cups all-purpose flour
- 2 ¼ tsp active yeast
- ¾ tbsp sugar
- 2 tsp salt
- 2 ½ tsp garlic powder
- 1 ½ cup warm water
- 2 tbsp olive oil
- 2 tbsp cilantro oil (Oil and Vinegar and Celia's online)
- ¼ cup shredded parmesan cheese
- ½ tsp sea salt

Instructions

- Coat a 9 by 13-inch pan with non-stick oil spray.

- In a large mixing bowl, measure the flour, oil, salt, yeast and water together. Beat with a mixer for about a minute.

- Transfer the dough into the oiled pan. Cover the pan lightly with plastic wrap. Let it rise for an hour at room temperature.

- After the dough has been resting for about 30 minutes, preheat the oven to 375 f. (190C)

- Once you have reached 60 minutes gently press dimples into the surface dough with your fingers.

- Drizzle olive oil and cilantro oil all over the top that way the oil can settle into the dimples.

- Sprinkle some flaky salt on top.

- Bake for 28-30 minutes or until golden brown.

- Remove from the oven and let cool on a rack for 5 minutes.

If you decide to use bread flour, increase the way by ¼ cup.

Make sure that you are using warm water. You want the water to be room temp.

I love this recipe because it is easy on the stomach and full of flavor. Sometimes I will make sandwiches for my family with this bread.

Garlic Oil infused mashed potatoes

I love garlic! In everything. I am Italian so it's in my DNA! If you are not a garlic fan, you do not need to put the infused garlic in your mashed potatoes. Make sure that you skin all of your potatoes. You may choose a dairy free option.

I have found that yellow potatoes are better on my stomach. I do switch it up to Russets as well. The option is yours.

 Serves about 4 depending on how much you love potatoes. I can eat a ton of them!

Ingredients

- 1.25 pounds of yellow of russet potatoes (skinned)
- 2 tbsp infused garlic oil (Oil and Vinegar or Celia's online)
- 2 ounces cream cheese (can be dairy free)
- 2 ounces sour cream (can be dairy free)
- Half stick of butter (I use vegan butter, you can also chose dairy free)
- Salt and pepper to taste

Instructions

- Grab a large pot, fill it with water and bring it to a boil

- Skin your potatoes and cut them into large chunks

- Place the potatoes in the pot of boiling water (be careful not to burn yourself)

- Cook them for 15 minutes (you want to make sure that the potatoes are tender, you do not want undercooked potatoes)

- Drain the water from the potatoes and put the potatoes back into the pot. Place back on the burner and add in all the ingredients.

- Mash up your potatoes. If you do not like chunky mashed potatoes, you can mash them until they are smooth.

- I love butter so I will add more butter to my potatoes once they are on my plate.

Potatoes are very easy to digest. Potatoes are mostly made up of insoluble fiber which speeds up digestion. Potatoes were one of the first things that I ate after my surgery. When I get a bowel obstruction, a little bit of mashed potatoes is what I eat when I start back on solid foods.

Ground Chicken Meatloaf

 Serves about 12 but if your family loves to eat, it's more like 6! One of my favorite things about this recipe is that you can make a mean meatloaf sandwich. I like to use sourdough bread, swiss cheese and a lot of mayo! You may choose gluten free and dairy free options.

Ingredients

- 2 pounds ground chicken
- ½ cup grated parmesan cheese
- ½ cup dried breadcrumbs
- 2 eggs
- 1 ½ tbsp onion powder
- 2 tbsp garlic powder
- 2 tbsp milk
- 1 tbsp worcestershire sauce
- ½ tsp salt
- ¼ teaspoon finely ground black pepper

The Glaze

- ½ cup ketchup
- ½ tbsp maple syrup
- 2 tbsp brown sugar
- ½ tsp onion powder
- ¼ tsp salt

Instructions

- Preheat oven to 375f (190C)

- Line a quarter size cooking sheet with foil

- Combine all of the ingredients for meatloaf in a large bowl. This is not including the glaze. The glaze is meant for the top of the meatloaf. Do not over mix.

- To prepare the glaze

- Mix all the glaze ingredients together. Make sure that the glaze is smooth.

- Shape the chicken meatloaf mixture into a 9 by 5-inch (23x12) loaf onto a baking dish.

- Spread the glaze evenly over the top of the meatloaf. Place meatloaf in the oven and cook for about 55 to 60 minutes. Or until the temperature reaches 165f (74c)

- Once done, remove the meatloaf from the oven and let it rest for about 10 minutes.

I like to serve this with homemade mashed potatoes. Make sure that if you are making mashed potatoes to skin them.

I also like to serve this with seasoned canned carrots. Both of these will be in the recipe book.

This is a wonderful dish to have at family get-togethers or if it's cold outside. Pretty simple to make and you will love the flavors.

Nutella and Sourdough

I love chocolate and I love nuts. Unfortunately for me and for people like me, nuts may be a big issue. I know that I cannot eat nuts or I will end up with a bowel obstruction and or in the hospital. When it comes to making this for my family, I add fruit like raspberries or cut up strawberries. You may choose a dairy free option.

This is one of the easiest recipes you could make. You can make it for breakfast or a dessert.

 Serves 1

Ingredients

- Nutella spread.
- Powdered sugar
- Sourdough (make sure it's true sourdough bread. It will state that there is a sourdough starter on the ingredients list)
- Strawberries and raspberries for those who can eat it

Instructions

- Turn your broiler on high, have your oven rack set closest to the broiler.

- Put the sourdough on a baking sheet. Add the Nutella spread. I always say the more the merrier.

- Put the cookie sheet in the broiler for about a minute. Until you see the Nutella start to turn brown. After the Nutella starts browning, take it out of the oven and put it on a plate. Add powdered sugar to taste. If you can eat the fruit, add the fruit and then the powdered sugar.

- There you go! You get a bit of protein; good carbs and it hits your taste buds!

Infused Garlic Air Fried Pasta Chips

Ingredients

- 1/2 pound rigatoni pasta with semolina (this pasta is better on the Gi tract) you may choose gluten free and dairy free options.
- 1 tbsp infused garlic oil (Oil and Vinegar and Celia's online)
- ½ tsp salt (if you don't like salty chips, don't add that much)
- Ground fine black pepper (optional)
- ½ cup grated parmesan cheese (can be dairy free)

Instructions

- Fill a large pan with water, and let it come to a boil. After the water has boiled, add your pasta to the water

- Cook for about 13 minutes

- After the pasta is done, drain the pasta. Put the pasta back into a larger bowl.

- Add in all the ingredients. Make sure to stir well so all of the pasta has seasoning on them.

- Air fryer 390 for 15 minutes

- Take the fried pasta out of the air fryer and place the pasta on a plate or bowl

and sprinkle the parmesan cheese on top.

I love this recipe because you know that it is going to taste well and that it is not going to hurt your stomach. I love chips but I must be careful because there cannot be skins or certain spices on them.

Lemon Cake

If you choose a gluten free option, please read the instructions. The instructions may differ from using regular flour.

Ingredients for cake

- 3 cups (345 grams) cake flour. Please make sure to level the flour. No more, no less than 3 cups.
- 2 tsp baking powder
- ½ tsp baking soda
- ½ tsp salt
- 1 cup buttermilk (240ml, room temperature)
- ¼ vegetable oil
- ¼ cup lemon juice (I buy mine from the store so there is no pulp)
- 2 tsp pure vanilla extract
- 1 cup (2 sticks) unsalted, softened butter
- 1 ¾ cups (350 grams) granulated sugar
- 4 large eggs (room temperature)

Ingredients for cream cheese frosting

- 12 ounces(340 grams) brick style cream cheese (softened)
- ¾ cup unsalted butter(1 ½ sticks of butter or 170 grams) softened
- 3 cups (360 grams) powdered sugar
- 2 tbsp lemon juice

Instructions for cake

- Preheat oven to 350f (180c)

- Spray non stick oil to 2, 9 inch round cake pans. Line the bottom of the pans with parchment paper.

- In a large mixing bowl, whisk cake flour, baking powder, baking soda, and salt together until well combined. Set it aside.

- In a separate large mixing bowl, whisk the buttermilk, oil, lemon juice, and vanilla extract together. Set aside

- If you have a mixer with a stand, use the paddle attachment, beat the butter on the low setting until the butter is smooth, then slowly add in the grated granulated sugar.

- Once all the sugar is added, increase the speed to medium. You want the mixture to be light and fluffy.

- Mix in the eggs one at a time. Make sure to stop and scrape the side of the mixing bowl after each egg.

- Add in the dry ingredients. You want to add this in 3 additions alternating with the buttermilk mixture. Make sure to mix at low speed. Mix in each addition until just combined. Make sure that you do not over mix the batter.

- If you have a rubber spatula use it to scrape around the bottom and the sides of the bowl to make sure that everything is combined.

- Evenly divide the cake batter between the 2 prepared cake pans and spread it around evenly.

- Bake the cake for 28 to 32 minutes. Use a toothpick to check the center to make sure that the toothpick comes out clean. Remove it from the oven and allow it to cool for 20 minutes. Then very carefully remove the cakes from the pans and let them cook completely.

Making of the Lemon Cream Frosting

- In a bowl or a mixer fiddle with a paddle or whisk, beat the cream cheese until it is smooth. Add the butter and mix for about 30 seconds, or until the ingredients are smooth.

- Add the powdered sugar and the lemon juice. Make sure to scrape the bottom and the sides. You want to make sure that the ingredients are fully combined.

Assembling the cake

- Level the tops of each cake the best that you can. You can use a knife or leveler. Place one of the cakes on a cake stand or a flat plate. Top with frosting. Place the second layer of cake on top of the other cake and cover the top and sides with frosting.

If you do not like frosting, you can opt for a strawberry compote. There is fruit in it. I remove the fruit and add the thick syrup. I sprinkle a little bit of powdered frosting on top.

I love this recipe because it does not contain fruit. I cannot eat fruit so being able to taste the lemon makes me smile.

You can add frosting or fruit that you like to make it as you wish. The foundation of the cake is already there for you.

Cilantro Rice

Ingredients

- 1 cup minute rice (rinse 3 to 4 times to clean the rice)
- 2 cups water
- 1 tsp salt
- 3 tbsp cilantro infused olive oil (Oil and Vinegar and Cela's online)
- 2 tbsp lemon juice
- 1 ½ tsp infused garlic olive oil

Instructions

- In a bowl, combine salt, cilantro oil, lemon juice, and garlic oil.

- Stir all of the ingredients together.

- Boil water

- Add rice, stir and cover for 5 minutes. After 5 minutes add the mixture from the bowl and stir well. Remove from stove top and let it sit for about a minute. That's it. This recipe gives you all of the flavors that you need without worry about chunky seasonings.

Benefits of rice

Rice is one of the easiest foods to digest. It typically takes around 30 to 120 minutes to digest rice. Make sure to chew chew, chew. The more you chew the easier it is for your body to digest the food.

Mama T's Potato Soup

This recipe is a crockpot recipe. You really want it to cook for 4-6 hours so the potatoes are nice and soft.

I know with me and my gut issues I cannot eat veggies or fruit. Every time I try, I end up with a bowel obstruction that lasts a week. There are 2 veggies that I can eat. Potatoes (no skin) and Carrots (peeled or canned is the best)

If your carrots aren't cooked all the way through, you will have digestion issues. So, I really do buy canned carrots. Known fact, Canned carrots have more nutrients than raw carrots. So, it's a win for me! You may choose a dairy free option.

 I cook for a family of 3. My husband can definitely eat.

Ingredients

- 4 large russet potatoes (skinless)
- 14.5 ounces canned carrots including liquid
- 40 ounces chicken broth
- 4 boneless skinless chicken thighs cut up into chunks
- 1/2 stick butter
- 1/2 tbsp garlic powder
- 1/2 tbsp onion powder
- 1/2 tbsp greek seasoning
- 12 oz evaporated milk (add 5 minutes before you serve, or it will curdle) dairy free options

Instructions

- In a large bowl add your dry seasoning to the chicken. Mix well.

- In your crock pot add your broth, potatoes and carrots. Add the chicken to your crockpot. Give it a good stir. Cut up you butter into chunks and add it to the crock pot.

- Cook on high for 4-6 hours. Add the evaporated milk to the crockpot 5 minutes before you eat. If you add it in after 5 minutes, there is a very good chance that it will start to curdle. Mix it well with the soup and there ya have it!

This is my family's favorite. It doesn't matter if it is cold or hot outside. This soup warms the soul. Simple and easy to throw in the crockpot and go about your day. My family and I like to broil some sourdough bread with butter and garlic salt. Just to the point where the bread is crisp. We dip our bread into the soup.

This Isn't Just Bone Broth

I know for me there are times that I literally cannot eat anything because my bowels have decided to not work, I have bacterial overgrowth, or I am having a bowel obstruction. When this happens, I cannot eat. I am on a clear liquid diet until my body starts working properly.

This is a broth recipe that will give you some nutrients and not be bland. You will have the sodium that you need to stay hydrated.

Ingredients

- Bone broth 32 ounces (can buy at any store)
- Extra fine mesh stainless steel Strainer (8")
- 1 tbsp. yellow onion (cut into chunks, not small)
- 1 whole garlic clove (peeled)

Instructions

- In a pot add 15 ounces of the bone broth. Heat up to medium heat.

- Put the chunks of onion and garlic clove inside the strainer.

- After the broth starts to heat, turn the burner on simmer for about 10 minutes.

- Add the onion and garlic in with the broth.

- After 10 minutes, pull out the strainer. Make sure that there are no loose pieces of onion floating in the broth. If that happens, strain the broth into another bowl.

That's it. You can sip on this broth throughout the day. I drink mine very hot because hot fluids help the bowel obstruction to pass.

There are many benefits of bone broth. Bone broth supports gut health, provides electrolytes and helps reduce inflammation. There are about 10 grams of protein in 1 cup of bone broth.

Parmesan Baked Potato Fries

You may choose a dairy free option.

 Serves about 3

Ingredients

- 3 Large yellow potatoes skinned and cut into wedges
- 2 tbsp olive oil
- ½ tbsp garlic powder
- ½ tbsp onion powder
- ½ tbsp slap ya mama seasoning (local grocery store sells this)
- 3 tbsp grated parmesan cheese
- Salt and pepper to taste

I like my fries with a lot of salt so this is all up to you!

Instructions

- Preheat oven to 450 f (230c)

- In a large bowl mix the seasonings in with the potato wedges. Let stand for a few minutes so the potatoes take in the flavor of the seasonings.

- Put parchment paper on a cookie sheet. Add the potatoes. Cook for 15 minutes.

- After 15 minutes, flip the wedges over. 3 minutes before the potatoes are done add the 3 tbsp of grated parmesan cheese. Close the oven door and let the wedges finish cooking.

I have a homemade fry sauce that I have included in this cookbook.

Salmon And Sourdough Sandwich

You may choose gluten free and dairy free options.

 Serving size 4

Ingredients

- 4 wild-caught Alaskan Sockeye Filets (boneless and skinless)
- 4 tbsp softened butter (can be dairy free)
- 1 tbsp olive oil
- 3 ½ tbsp lemon juice
- 2 tsp garlic powder
- 2 tbsp fish sauce
- ½ tbsp soy sauce
- 1 tsp old bay seasoning (local grocery store)
- 4 pieces of large sourdough bread cut in half (gluten free bread is fine)
- Mayo (as much as you like, this is for the sourdough)
- 4 slices of swiss or gouda cheese (can be dairy free)

Instructions

- In a large bowl add all the ingredients, mix well. Add the boneless, skinless salmon to the bowl. With your hands, coat the fish with the ingredients. Cover with plastic wrap and set in the fridge for 10 minutes, you want the seasonings to marry with the fish.

- In a large frying pan or cast-iron skillet, add the olive oil. Have the heat set from low to medium. After the oil is warm add the fish. Cook the fish for 2 to 3 minutes on each side.

- After the salmon is done, take a slice of cheese and set it on top of the salmon. Turn the heat off and let the cheese melt.

- Turn your broiler on high

- Add your sliced up sourdough to a cooking sheet. Once the sourdough is placed on the cooking sheet, you want to evenly coat the bread with butter.

- Put the sourdough in the oven and let it broil for a minute or until the bread starts to get crispy. Flip the bread over and put back in the broiler for another minute.

- Pull the bread out of the oven and set the bread on a plate. Add as much mayo that you would like. Add the salmon to the bread. Put the other slice of bread on top of the salmon.

If you are making this for other people, you can add lettuce and some slices of yellow onion. It gives the sandwich a little extra crunch.

Sal-mon Filets

Salmon is one of the best things that we can put in our bodies. Fish is very easy to digest. Make sure that when you buy salmon that it is boneless and skinless. We eat all different types of fish. May choose dairy free options.

Ingredients

 This recipe is for 2, 5 ounce filets of salmon. If you are making more than 1 piece, double up on the seasoning.

- 2 1/2 tbsp olive oil
- 3 tbsp lemon juice (I buy RealLemon at the local grocery store)
- ½ tbsp fish sauce (I buy Thai kitchen at the local grocery store)
- 1 tsp soy sauce
- ½ tbsp old bay seasoning
- 2 tbsp vegan butter (you can use any kind you like
- Add salt to taste!

Instructions

- On medium heat cook for 2 minutes on each side so 4 minutes total. This really depends on the thickness of the salmon. We buy freshwater boneless and skinless salmon, so it cooks somewhat fast. The thicker the salmon, the longer it takes.

Fun fact

It takes approximately 30 minutes to digest salmon. The fattier the salmon the longer it takes to digest.

Salmon reduces inflammation, lowers cholesterol levels, maintains blood pressure and prevents excess fluid retention. Salmon is heart healthy full of Omega 3 fatty acids.

Shrimp Stir Fry 2 ways.

I love seafood. I love shrimp. I do have to make sure that the shrimp that I am eating is cooked perfectly. If it is cooked too long it is hard and my body struggles to digest the food. If the shrimp isn't cooked enough, it is very chewy and let's be honest, no one likes that.

I am going to split this up into 2 recipes. A recipe for us who cannot eat all the veggies and a recipe for those who can eat all of the goodies.

Let's be honest, all rice is not equal. There are many types of rice that I can not eat. My body struggles hard. But Minute made white rice is literally my best friend. I do not have any issues with this rice. Side note, make sure that you rinse the rice in water 3 times. It removes most of the starch and makes it easier to digest.

You can choose to buy frozen veined and peeled shrimp, or you can buy fresh shrimp and do it yourself. Depending on how I am feeling, I will decide if I want to make it simple or if I want to take the time out and really get into it.

Gut Friendly version

Ingredients

- ½ cup equals 1 serving size. I usually make enough for 4 people.
- 2 cups Minute Rice white rice
- 2 large eggs
- 16 ounces of frozen or fresh shrimp
- 3 tbsp infused Cilantro garlic oil (Oil and Vinegar and Celia's sells this online)
- 1 tbsp Old Bay seasoning
- ½ tbsp garlic powder
- ½ tbsp onion powder
- ¼ cup vegan butter (you can use any butter you like)
- 2 tbsp fish sauce (I prefer Thai Kitchen; most stores sell this)
- 1 tbsp olive oil

Instructions

Rice

- After reading and cooking the minute rice from the instructions label, put your rice in the fridge and let it cool down. Keep the rice in the fridge for 15 to 20 minutes. Once the rice has cooled down, grab a large frying pan. Add oil to the pan. I set my temperature to medium high. Once the pan is hot, add in the rice. Once the rice starts to get crispy you want to add in 2 eggs and stir it in with the rice.

Shrimp

- If you are using frozen shrimp, please allow the shrimp to cook for a good 10 to 12 minutes. If you are using fresh shrimp, it usually takes 5 to 7 minutes to cook.

- In a large bowl, add your shrimp along with all of the ingredients minus the 2 eggs. Once mixed set aside. In a separate frying pan add some water and olive oil. Once the pan is hot cook your shrimp. Once the shrimp is done, add the shrimp to the rice. Mix well. You can add more soy sauce if you like your stir fry saucy!

Veggies (Not gut friendly)

- If you are going to add veggies to the stir fry, add them with the shrimp. You do not want to overcook your veggies. They will cook a bit more once you add all the ingredients together. You want your veggies to have a little crisp to them.

Simple breakfast packed with protein

Ingredients

Smoked salmon (prepackaged is fine) make sure that there is no skin on the smoked salmon that you purchase. You may choose gluten free and dairy free options.

- 1 large egg
- 1 half English muffin (may choose gluten free)
- 1 tbsp butter (may be dairy free)
- ½ tbsp infused cilantro oil (Oil and Vinegar and Celia's online)
- Salt and pepper to taste
- I like my English muffin very crispy. Please cook your muffin as you like it.
- Mayo (optional)

Instructions

- Heat a skillet over medium heat

- Add a little butter or olive oil to pan

- Crack the egg in a pan and let it cook for 3 minutes uncovered

- Add a lid and cover the egg for another 2 to 3 minutes. This will allow the whites of the egg to start cooking without the yoke over cooking.

- On a separate burner, on medium high, add in the cilantro, a little butter, salt and pepper. Put the half of the English muffin faced down, let it fry for a few minutes. Flip over.

- Once the English muffin is as crispy as you like, put on a plate, add the egg and smoked salmon and mayo

You have a protein packed breakfast. Simple yet delicious. If you do not like mayo, you can mash up some avocado and put it on your bread. Make sure that your avocado is not hard.

Spicy Rice Noodles

Ingredients

- 8 ounces wide rice noodles
- 4 tbsp infused garlic olive oil (Oil and Vinegar and Celia's online)
- 1 tbsp infused ginger olive oil (Oil and vinegar and Celia's online)
- 1 tbsp olive oil
- 4-5 tbsp low sodium soy sauce
- 1-3 tbsp infused chili or chipotle olive oil (Celia's online)
- 1 tbsp sriracha
- 2 tsp rice vinegar (any Asian market or grocery store)

 This recipe serves 4 but if you are like me and love noodles, you'll need to make more.

Instructions

- Bring a large pot of water to a boil. The cooking instructions are on the package instructions.

- In a large bowl all the seasonings together and mix well.

- When the noodles are done, combine the seasonings with the rice and mix well. Let simmer for a few minutes to allow the noodles to absorb all the flavor. You can add and remove any seasonings that you'd like to.

I love this recipe because you aren't missing any flavor. You get a little sweet from the rice vinegar, you get a little salt from the soy sauce, and you get flavor from the oils. For me, not having flavor really made me depressed. This recipe is something that you can make for yourself or for others. They will definitely request this when they come over.

Sugar Cooks (cookies)

You may choose gluten free and dairy free options. If you are choosing gluten free, please read the directions on the packaging.

 Makes around 30 cookies

Ingredients

- 1 cup butter (softened)
- 1 ¼ cups granulated sugar
- 1 egg
- 2 tsp vanilla extract
- 2 ½ cups all-purpose flour
- ½ tsp baking soda
- ½ tsp baking powder
- ¼ tsp salt

For top of cookies

- ¼ cup granulated sugar

Instructions

- Preheat oven to 350f (176c)

- Line a baking sheet with parchment paper or cooking spray

- In a large bowl or with a standing mixer or hand mixer, mix together the butter until creamy and add the sugar. Mix for about a minute until the mix is smooth.

- Add the egg, vanilla extract and beat together until combined.

- Add the flour, baking soda, baking powder, and salt. Mix until it is just combined. Make sure to scrape the bottom and the sides of the bowl.

- Roll the dough into 1-inch balls. After each ball is rolled, roll them in some of the granulated sugar you have for the tops of the cookies.

- Place the cookies on the baking sheet 2-inches apart

- Bake for about 9 to 11 minutes, or until the cookies have turned a light brown.

- Once you pull the cookies out of the oven, take them off the cookie sheet so they do not overcook.

- Let stand for a few minutes before serving.

One of my favorite things to do is dip my cookies in coffee with creamer. I can't stomach black coffee. If I don't add creamer, I get really bad heartburn. If you notice that you get heartburn after you drink coffee, drink less and add a little milk or creamer. The milk helps neutralize the acid from the coffee.

Wild Caught Lemon and Garlic Alaskan Sockeye Filets

This recipe is delicious. One of the things that I love to pair with this salmon is my Cilantro rice. You won't have to look very far because this recipe is in this book! You may choose a gluten free option.

 This recipe is for 4 people.

Ingredients

- 4 wild-caught Alaskan Sockeye Filets (boneless and skinless)
- 4 tbsp softened butter (unsalted)
- 3 ½ tbsp lemon juice
- 2 tsp garlic powder
- 1 tbsp infused cilantro oil (Oil and Vinegar or Celia's online)

Instructions

- In a bowl combine all the ingredients and mix well

- Preheat oven to 375f (200c)

- Place the salmon filets on a baking sheet lined with parchment paper.

- Spread the butter mixture evenly over the salmon filets.

- Bake the Salmon in the preheated oven for about 12-15 minutes until the salmon is cooked all the way through.

Wild-caught salmon is fished out of natural habitats at various locations throughout the entire world. Farmed fish are raised in an aquaculture environment. One of the biggest differences that I have noticed is the fat content. There is less fat on the Wild-caught salmon. I do love both fishes, so when I make my homemade fish soup, I use the farm raised salmon. Depending on the store that you purchase your salmon at, they may not be skinned. You can ask at the counter if they will skin it for you or you can do it yourself. You can also purchase these prepackaged and frozen.

Wasabi Deviled Eggs

Ingredients

- 12 large eggs (see boiling instructions below)
- ½ cup mayo
- 1 tbsp yellow mustard
- 2 ½ tsp wasabi sauce
- 1 ½ tsp garlic powders
- 1 tsp onion powder
- Salt and pepper to taste

Instructions

- I have learned that if you put a little vinegar in the water while boiling your eggs, the shells come off a lot easier.

- In a large pot including a lid if you have one (if not, no big deal) add cold water. Add in the eggs. Bring the eggs and the water to a boil. Turn off the stove and then place the lid over the pot. Let the eggs sit for 10 to 12 minutes. I always drain the water and add ice and water to the eggs. This helps them cool off faster.

- After the eggs are cooled off, peel them. I start peeling the bottom part of the egg first. It breaks the little sack that is inside which makes the eggs peel better.

- After you peel your eggs, cut them in half. Put the yoke part of the eggs in a separate bowl. Do this to all of your eggs.

- After you have all of the yoke in a bowl, add the ingredients. Make sure to mix well. If you want a creamier consistency you can add more mayo.

- Fill the eggs with the filling.

I love the creamy, salty flavor with a little kick. If I have any left-over filling, I will save it and make a sandwich. It's delicious.

Eggs are a wonderful source of protein. Now hard-boiled eggs can be hard on some stomachs. Some people can eat fried eggs and scrambled eggs but hard boiled eggs bother them. So start with eating half of one to see if your body will tolerate it. If 15 minutes goes by and you have no issues, you should be good to go!

The Best Steak That You Will Ever Have

This recipe is not intended for people who cannot eat red meat. If you struggle with meat, please do not try to eat this. The last thing that I want is for you to have more stomach issues on top of the ones that you already have.

Fact... Red meat is one of the hardest foods for your body to digest. In general, it takes 2-3 hours for the meat to leave the stomach and be fully digested in 4-6 hours. The meat in your stomach actually starts to rot. Don't get me wrong. I grew up eating steak. I love the flavor and miss eating it but, I will not chance ever eating it again. Please use your own discretion when it comes to eating any red meat.

 Serving size 2

Ingredients

- 2 boneless ribeye steaks with fat on them
- Meat tenderizer
- Onion powder
- Garlic powder
- Salt and pepper to taste
- 2 pieces of sage
- Butter (can be dairy free)
- Worcestershire sauce

Instructions

- 10 minutes before you start cooking your steaks, set out the steaks and season them. You want to give some time for your steaks to not be so cold.

- Mix all of the ingredients minus steaks and sage in a large dish. Coat all sides of the steaks.

- Put your steaks in the pan and put the sage in between the steaks. If you are broiling them, make sure to use an oven safe cooking pan or baking sheet.

Cooking times

Frying pan

- Rare steaks (115f-120f) 2 minutes each side
- Medium (120f-125f) 3 minutes each side
- Medium rare (125f-135f) 4 minutes each side
- Medium well (135f-145f) 5 minutes each side

Cooking times to broil in oven

- The steaks should be 2-4 inches away from the broiler. Set broiler temperature to high

- Rare steaks 6-10 minutes
- Medium rare 10-12 minutes
- Medium well 12-14 minutes
- Well 14-16 minutes

Make sure to flip your steaks every 3 minutes, you want to make sure that they are cooking evenly on both sides.

When you pull your steaks from the stove top of the broiler, put them in a separate plate and let them rest. I will put a little butter on top of the steak and let it melt. Pour the remaining juices from the pans onto the steaks. Cover the steaks with tin foil. It is important to cover the steaks as this will lock in the juices. After letting the steaks rest for 10 minutes, they are ready to eat!

Cucumber salad

This salad is not intended for people who can't eat raw cucumbers or tomatoes. Please be advised that if you do eat this, there is a chance that you will have a bowel obstruction. If you can eat this, I hope that you enjoy it!

Ingredients

- 1 large English cucumber
- ½ steak tomato cut into chunks
- ¼ cup finely chopped onion (yellow or purple)
- ½ cup sour cream (may be dairy free)
- ½ tsp dill
- Salt and pepper to taste

Instructions

- You decide if you want to peel the cucumber skin off or you can keep it on there.

- Do not cut your cucumber in half. Cut your cucumber in thin pieces.

- Cut your tomato into little chunks

- Cut your onion into little chunks

- In a large bowl, add your sour cream, dill, salt and pepper. Mix well. After the mixture is smooth, add your vegetables. Stir well. Cover and put into the fridge until you are ready to serve.

Did you say fruit to my salad?

This salad is for anyone who can eat fruit and vegetables.

Although I cannot eat this salad, my family loves it and says that it is better than the store bought or salad that you would get at a restaurant.

Ingredients

 This salad is for a family of 2 or 3.

- 1 half yellow onion cut up into chunks
- 1 garlic clove cut up into chunks
- 1 larger cucumber cut into chunks
- 1 large tomato cut into chunks
- 4 mini sweet peppers cut into thin slices
- 4 strawberries cut into thin slices
- 1 tbsp olive oil
- ½ tsp balsamic vinegar
- 1 tsp fig glaze (DeNigris fig glaze, I buy at Walmart or Safeway) there are no chunks of fig, it is liquid form.
- Salt and pepper to taste

Instructions

- In a large mixing bowl add all of the ingredients together and there you have it, you have a wonderful salad full of flavor!

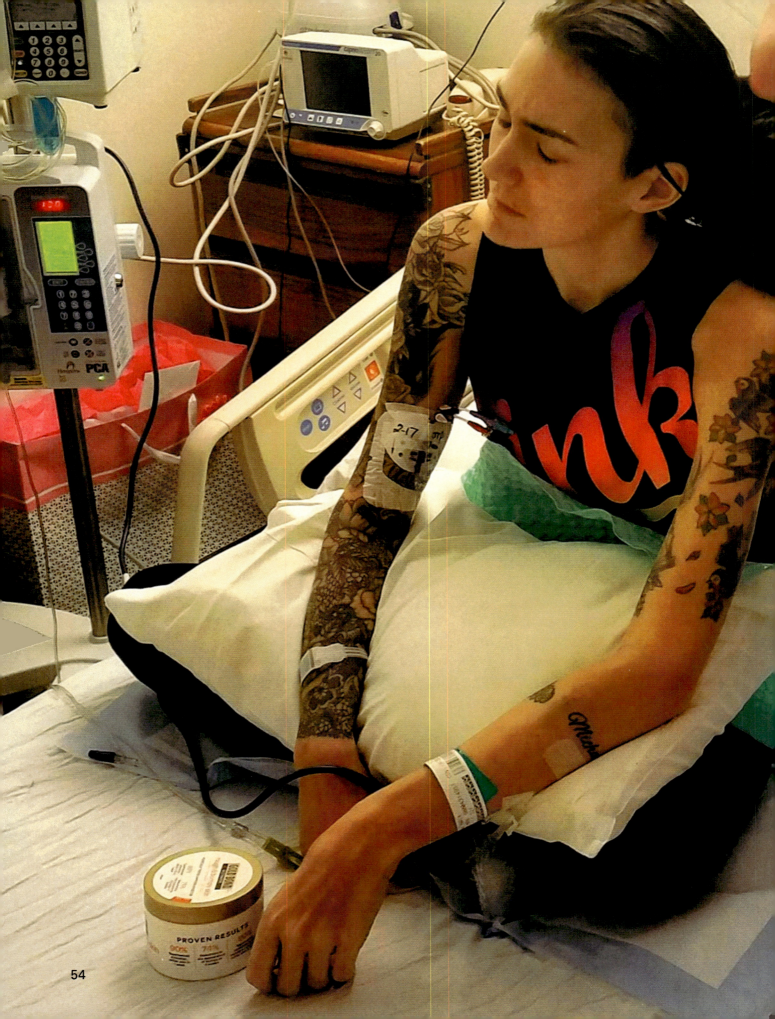

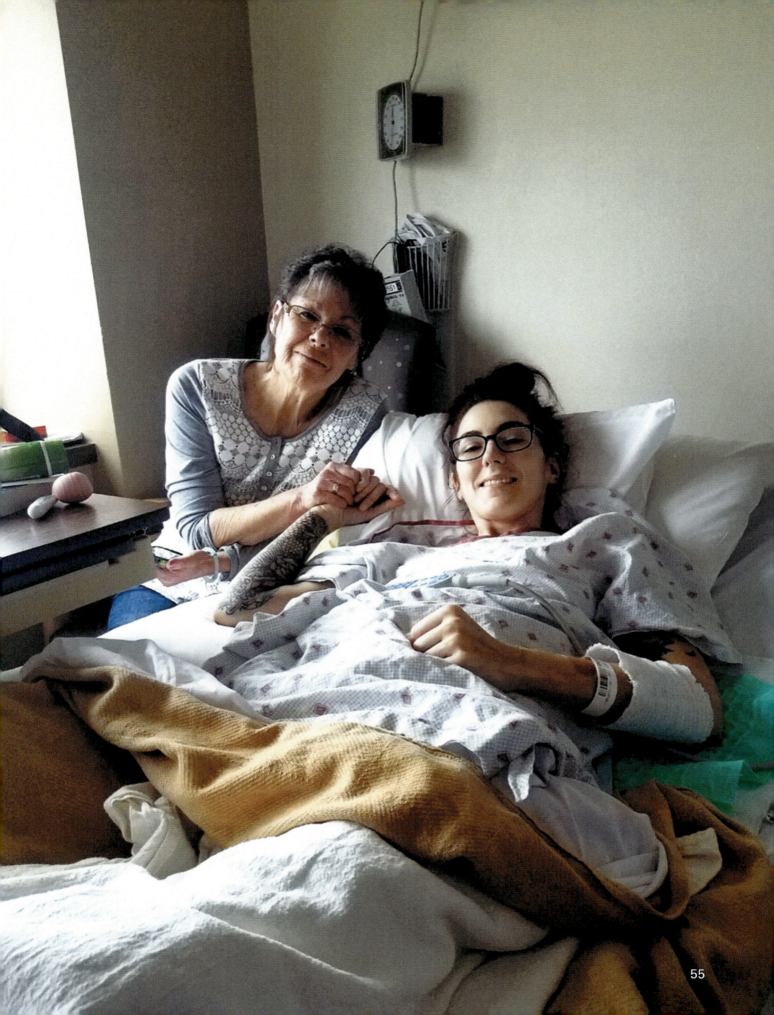

Printed in the United States
by Baker & Taylor Publisher Services